When Mom and Dad Divorce

A Kid's Resource

Written by
Emily Menendez-Aponte

Illustrated by
R. W. Alley

ONE
CARING
PLACE

Abbey Press
St. Meinrad, IN 47577

For my husband, Carlos,
and all of my parents—
Mom, Dad, Lisa, and John—
thank you for all of your love.

Text © 1999 Emily Menendez-Aponte
Illustrations © 1999 St. Meinrad Archabbey
Published by One Caring Place
Abbey Press
St. Meinrad, Indiana 47577

Library of Congress Catalog Number
99-76078

ISBN 0-87029-333-8

Printed in the United States of America

A Message to Parents, Teachers, and Other Caring Adults

Divorce is a difficult experience for any child. But the support of loving adults can make this passage much easier to navigate.

Parents need to tell children about an impending divorce or separation as soon as it is definite. Children pick up on family tensions and know intuitively that something is going on. Telling them honestly what is actually happening prevents them from imagining an even worse scenario.

Divorce can create a whirlwind of emotions for a child. It is critical to allow your child to experience and express those emotions. Repeatedly reassure her that you love her, that she is not in any way responsible for the divorce, and that you will always take care of her.

Change of any kind is difficult for most children, and divorce brings about monumental changes in a child's life. Parents need to carefully explain the logistics of the schedule, making sure everything is clear and understandable. Try to keep things consistent and predictable. Children generally do better if they know what to expect.

Although it's very natural for ex-spouses to have negative opinions toward one another, parents should refrain from expressing these opinions in front of their child. Regardless of how you feel toward your ex-spouse, this person is your child's parent. Your child still loves and needs both of you as parents. Negative opinions and comments will only create feelings of confusion and guilt for your child.

I hope that this book can be a vehicle to help your child start to understand and adjust to the changes in his life. Read this book with him; use it as a tool to begin talking and exploring feelings.

Give your child time to adjust to the radical changes that divorce brings. Though divorce is painful for all involved, it does not have to be permanently devastating. With cooperation, consistency, and continual love and encouragement, you can help your child make it through.

—*Emily Menendez-Aponte*

Lots of Things Are Changing

When your mom and dad get a divorce, it may feel like your life has just been turned upside-down. It's hard to think that the two people in the world who you love most don't love each other anymore.

So many things are changing all at once. In the middle of everything, you may wonder: "What's going to happen to ME?" Tell your parents what you wonder and worry about.

It's Not Your Fault

Parents get divorced for lots of different reasons—grown-up reasons. You may have seen or heard your parents fighting. They may have loud fights, or they may have quiet fights and not talk to each other much.

Whatever the reason for your parents' divorce, IT'S NOT YOUR FAULT. Your parents aren't getting divorced because you did something wrong. And there is nothing you can do better or differently to keep them from getting divorced. Sometimes it's just better for parents not to be married to each other anymore.

Your Parents Still Love You

Many things in your life are changing right now, but one thing will always stay the same—your parents will always love you.

Even if one of your parents doesn't live in the same house as you, you still have a mom and a dad. You still have two parents to love and care for you.

Though your parents may not love each other anymore, they both still love you very much. Parents only divorce each other. They don't divorce you!

All of Your Feelings

You might have all kinds of different feelings about what's happening in your life. You may be really angry, upset, or sad. Or maybe you are scared, worried, or confused.

It's okay to have these feelings—whatever they are. Many kids whose parents are going through a divorce have these same kinds of feelings.

Let yourself feel the way you feel. Talk about it with your mom or dad. It will take some time to sort through all your feelings.

Feeling Better

Remember that it's okay to cry when you are upset. Letting your feelings out can help you to feel better.

Doing things you like might also help you feel better. Drawing or playing with a favorite toy can help. Hugs can help, too. When you are upset, get a big hug from someone you love.

Talk to People

It's good to talk to people about what you are feeling. It's not good to keep all of your feelings hidden inside you.

Besides your mom or dad, it might help to talk with other grown-ups in your life, like a grandparent or teacher.

Your mom or dad might ask you to talk to a "counselor." A counselor is someone who helps people with their problems. You don't need to be embarrassed. Counselors are very good at listening and they can really help.

Your Parents Will Feel Sad, Too

Your mom and dad will probably feel sad about getting divorced, too. This might seem confusing to you, since they are the ones who decided to get divorced. You might see them cry or get upset and angry.

Giving a hug can help. But it's not your job to take care of your parents' feelings. Their feelings are not your fault. You can't stop your mom or dad from being upset.

Wishing

Just as you didn't do anything to make your parents get a divorce, you can't do anything to get them back together again.

Sometimes you might wish or pray that your parents would get married again. This probably won't happen. Parents who get a divorce usually don't get back together again.

But you can pray to God to help you handle your feelings. God wants to help you feel better.

Talking to Your Friends

Sometimes kids feel embarrassed that their parents are divorced. You may be ashamed that your family is "different." You might be afraid to tell your friends.

Though it's hard to tell your friends, it's better to let them know what's going on in your life. It may be easier to tell one friend at a time. You'll probably be surprised to find out you are not the only one whose parents are divorced.

Living at Different Places

Now your mom and dad will be living in two different homes. The time you spend with each of them will depend on what they decide works out best for all of you.

You'll probably live at both houses at least some of the time. This will take awhile to get used to. It can be easier if you keep some special things at each house—like favorite toys or pictures.

Sometimes it might be hard to keep track of where you are and where you need to be, and what clothes and other things you need. Let your parents know if it's too confusing for you. Together you can figure out a better way to keep track of things.

Working Things Out

Sometimes it might seem like you are in the middle of a tug-of-war between your parents. You feel pulled in two directions at once. You may especially feel this way on holidays or at special times, like your birthday.

Let your mom and dad know if you are feeling torn between the two of them. They don't want you to feel bad and can try to work things out to make it easier on you.

Or, if one of your parents says something bad about the other, you may be angry and sad. It hurts your feelings. Tell your parents that you don't like this, because you love them both.

It's Okay to Have Fun

There may be times when you are with your mom and wonder what your dad is doing, or when you're with your dad and miss your mom. You may worry about the parent who's not there, or even feel guilty about having fun without that person.

It's okay to have a good time and be happy. Your mom and dad want you to have fun and love both of them. It might help you to feel better if you call your mom or draw your dad a picture.

New People in Your Life

Your mom and dad will probably make new friends. They may go out on dates with other people. You might not like this at first. It may seem like it's not right or not fair to your other parent.

But your parents want to feel better, too. They want to meet new people and make new friends. It will help if you can think of at least one thing you like about your parent's new friend.

Eventually, your mom or dad might even get married to someone else. This new person will never take the place of your other parent, but will be another person in your life to love you and care about you.

Things Will Get Better

Divorce is a really hard thing for everyone in a family. Many things about your life will change and your family will be different. But different isn't always bad. Little by little, things will get better. Slowly, you will get used to the changes in your life—and there might even be some that you really like.

Always remember that your mom and dad love you very, very much. The love between you can reach from one house to another. It's something to think about when you feel upset or lonely. It will help you to get past this hard time to a happier time in the days to come.

Emily Menendez-Aponte holds a B.A. in Psychology and a Master of Social Work degree. As a licensed social worker, she has counseled families and children and has been trained as a divorce mediator. Currently she lives in New Jersey with her husband and is the director of a family mentoring program for a national nonprofit agency.

R.W. Alley is the illustrator for the popular adult and children's series of Elf-help books. He is also author-illustrator of a number of other children's books. He lives in Barrington, Rhode Island, with his wife, daughter, and son.